The War of the Sicilian Vespers: The History and Legacy of Sicily's Rebellion against the French in the Late 13th Century

By Charles River Editors

The Sicilian Vespers by Francesco Hayez (1846)

About Charles River Editors

Charles River Editors provides superior editing and original writing services across the digital publishing industry, with the expertise to create digital content for publishers across a vast range of subject matter. In addition to providing original digital content for third party publishers, we also republish civilization's greatest literary works, bringing them to new generations of readers via ebooks.

Sign up here to receive updates about free books as we publish them, and visit Our Kindle Author Page to browse today's free promotions and our most recently published Kindle titles.

Introduction

***The Sicilian Vespers* by Francesco Hayez**

It is hard to find an island on the map more central than Sicily. Located at the crossroads between Europe and Africa, and between the Eastern and Western Mediterranean, Sicily has rarely been governed as an independent, unified state. Nonetheless, the island has always occupied a front-row seat to some of the most important events in history, and nowhere is this more obvious than during antiquity.

Very fertile in ancient times, Sicily was especially prized for its grain production. The island had been inhabited by native tribes since prehistoric times, but by the 9th and 8th centuries BCE, Sicily would be the staging area for a confrontation between the Greeks and the Phoenicians, seafaring powers that scrambled to establish colonies along its coasts. These colonies, in time, would grow independent, and by the Classical era (510-323 BCE), they would be waging wars of their own.

It was during the Classical era that Sicily came the closest to being governed as a single, unified, and independent state. In time, it came to challenge the powerful trade empire of Carthage, a former Phoenician colony in North Africa, and it vied with the cities and kingdoms of mainland Greece for primacy in the Greek world. Later on, Sicily would be both a prize and a battlefield during the First Punic War (263-241 BCE) and, to a lesser degree, also during the Second Punic War (218-201 BCE). These were massive, protracted conflicts between Carthage and the rising Roman Republic, and Rome would subsequently become the main power in the Mediterranean on its way to ruling much of the known world. Sicily would go on to become the Roman Republic's first territory outside of Italy and its first province; and Hieron, the tyrant of Syracuse at the time, would be Rome's first client king. Thus, the two different models through which Rome would control its empire in the future made their first appearance in Sicily. The province of Sicily would furthermore be crucial when it came to providing funds, and especially grain, to the rising Roman Republic. Sicily would remain a Roman domain until the end of antiquity, and affairs on the island dramatically affected the Romans at home.

The largest island of the Mediterranean has always been a complicated place with a fraught relationship to the Italian mainland. Separated by only the narrow Strait of Messina, Sicily feels like a different country in many ways, and the differences between Sicilians and Italians are much vaster than the tiny geographical separating them might intimate. For example, the linguistic differences between the two are substantial, as Sicilian is practically its own language, rather than just a dialect. In fact, most Italians have difficulty understanding Sicilian if they can comprehend any of it at all.

There is also an ethnic difference between Sicilians and Italians. Most notably, many Sicilians have bright red hair and light eyes, which is usually thought to be a result of the Norman invasions, although today some historians believe it is because of the strong presence of the British during the Napoleonic Wars, as well as the Anglo-American occupation of Italy during World War II. Even Sicilian cuisine varies from the Italian mainland - Sicily is celebrated for having 72 different kinds of bread, and Sicilians often eat ice cream (gelato) for breakfast.

However diverse Sicily might be, it is also paradoxically considered to be an emblem of Italy itself, a paradox it shares with Naples. In fact, Frederick II was the last ruler of a fully autonomous Sicily, and his son, Manfred (r. 1254-1258), was the final Norman ruler in Sicily. Manfred met his death heroically on the battlefield, fighting the army of Charles of Anjou after Charles was made King of Rome by the Vatican in 1266.[1] Charles chose Naples as the capital of his lands, and this created tensions between his people and the Sicilians, culminating with a rebellion known as the Sicilian Vespers of 1282. According to legend, the rebellion started after a French soldier harassed a Sicilian woman on Easter Sunday outside the Church of Santo Spirito.

When it started, the rebellion inaugurated a period of anarchy in Sicily, and for a time was unclear who would take the crown. Two warring factions, the Aragonese and the Angevins, competed for the crown for 90 years, to the detriment of all involved. At one point, there were two different kings of Sicily, one from each side, and it was not until 1372 that peace was finally reached and the Aragonese were awarded rule of Sicily. As a result of all this geopolitical turmoil, Sicily's status in the world was greatly diminished. Spain was on the rise, and even if Palermo received certain bureaucratic dispensations,

---

[1] Monroe, 80-81.

nothing would shift the center of power back into Sicily's orbit. [2]

In the wake of the infighting, Sicily was affected by other major geopolitical events elsewhere. When Constantinople fell in 1453, the ascent of the Ottoman Turks meant that Sicily was constantly being threatened. Pirates and corsairs from North Africa continued to besiege the coastal towns, and the island became an important staging ground for those trying to counter the Muslims.[3] Thus, while much of Europe experienced a flourishing culture during the Renaissance, the 15th and 16th centuries in Sicily were completely cut off from all the cultural and technological advances, despite the fact Italy was the epicenter of everything. Moreover, thanks to Spain's Catholic zeal, Sicily faced the worst excesses of the Counter-Reformation.[4]

The War of the Sicilian Vespers: The History and Legacy of Sicily's Rebellion against the French in the Late 13th Century chronicles the revolt and the ensuing war that was fought among several European powers. Along with pictures of important people, places, and events, you will learn about the War of the Sicilian Vespers like never before.

---

[2] Farrell, *Sicily: A Cultural History*.

[3] For example, the Christian fleet departed from Messina, Sicily, in 1453, on their way to fight in the important Battle of Lepanto against the Turks.

[4] Farrell, Sicily: A Cultural History.

The War of the Sicilian Vespers: The History and Legacy of Sicily's Rebellion against the French in the Late 13th Century

Medieval Sicily

Roman power in Sicily was consolidated after the Second Punic War, and Sicily remained under Rome's thumb for the entire imperial period, roughly until the Vandals started making incursions from Africa in the mid-5th century CE and damaged the island's political and economic ties to Rome. The Romans would still hold on to Sicily for a little while longer, particularly because of land ties between the island and the Church, but Roman control was no longer unequivocal.

Naturally, the fall of the Roman Empire marked a period of great change for the Sicilians, as it did for all the groups who had been part of the empire. As a result, they were subjugated by a number of foreign rulers, including Germanic groups and Ostrogoths, until the Byzantines under Justinian the Great sought to reunify the lost Roman Empire.

A contemporary mosaic depicting Justinian I

   As for Justinian's great schemes for uniting both halves of the once great Roman Empire, things did not turn out as planned. Though he had conquered Italy, Northern Africa, and the greater portion of Gaul with the help of Belisarius and Narses, he decimated both his royal coffers and his armies in doing so. His constant war against the nations he perceived as obstacles for his plans demanded a constant influx of soldiers, and he had supplemented his ranks by retrieving troops from the Danube *limitanei* stations and leaving the northern frontier vulnerable to attacks by the Avars and Slavs. The increased taxes he imposed on the local population, who retaliated by fleeing and joining the barbarian troops instead of cultivating the land, made things even worse.

In the end, the attempt to reunite the empires was probably a futile task if only because the religious and cultural divisions that had come into existence long before were too great to be filled with an administrative merger. However, during this time, Sicily was a crossroads whose shores welcomed a variety of figures, from pilgrims, warriors, and saints to messengers and administrators, as well as immigrants looking to settle.[5] The Byzantines made eastern Siracusa the regional capital and deported many of its native inhabitants to Naples. Emperor Justinian also changed life in Sicily by devising a legal code which he imposed on the entire island, with the goal of making each of the provinces able to practice self-government. The Byzantines imported administrators, soldiers, and monks to help consolidate their power. The monks brought a formal curriculum to the island, teaching the Sicilian youth about Greek philosophy, rhetoric and

---

[5] Davis-Secord, chapter 1.

music. The Byzantines also began changing the architecture of the houses of worship on the island, bringing their signature brightly colored mosaics to adorn the newly built churches.[6]

Although the Byzantines were initially more appreciated by the Sicilians than the Romans had been, inevitably this relationship soon began to sour. The Byzantine customs (such as an insistence on covering the entire body, even in extreme heat) were incompatible with the Sicilian way of life. They instituted repressive policies against women, and their pedagogical techniques were focused on rote memorization rather than open questioning. Perhaps most emblematic of all, their beloved Greek god, Dionysus, the patron saint of theater and fun, was transformed by the Byzantines into a hellish creature, and the Byzantines tried to repress any associated festivities that were important to Sicilian culture, even going so far as to refuse to baptize actors.[7]

As Byzantine power in the region faltered, Sicily became susceptible to Arab invasions, which started with random acts of piracy.[8] In 652, a small force of Muslims began to make incursions in Sicily, but while they were fierce and determined, they still lacked the formal organization to

---

[6] Benjamin, chapter 3. On the mosaics, see Adele Cilento, *Byzantine Mosaics in Norman Sicily* (Reggio Emilia, IT: Magnus Edizioni SpA, 2019).

[7] Benjamin, chapter 3.

[8] Karla Mallette, *The Kingdom of Sicily, 1100-1250: A Literary History* (Philadelphia, PA: University of Pennsylvania Press, 2011), 5.

actually take any cities or do real damage.[9] However, by 827, the expansionist Muslims were capable of a full-blown military operation, and it would only take three years for the Arabs to take the island, with Palermo falling in 830. What they found when they took over was a culture in a profoundly decaying state.[10] The east coast city of Syracuse, which was the last main Christian outpost on the island of Sicily, held out for a longer period of time, lasting until 878 before falling to the Arab invaders.

These initial years of Muslim rule marked a turbulent period for the inhabitants of Sicily, both because of the struggles faced by the Muslim world at this time and because of their own internal conflicts.[11] After these conflicts started to die down, however, Muslim Sicily entered into a period of peace and prosperity, considered by some historians to be a cultural "golden age" for the island.[12]

Then, just as abruptly as it had started, the Arab rule of Sicily ended. The first Norman invaders arrived in Sicily in 1038, after the Arab population had already ruled the island for about 200 years.[13] The Normans originally

---

[9] Benjamin, chapter 3.

[10] Karla Mallette, *The Kingdom of Sicily, 1100-1250: A Literary History* (Philadelphia, PA: University of Pennsylvania Press, 2011), 5.

[11] Mallette, 4.

[12] Mallette, 5.

[13] Mallette, 4. On the Normans, see also Mariano Marrone, *Il regno di Sicilia: dai Normanni agli Aragonesi* (Chieti, IT: Solfanelli Editore, 2014).

came to Italy and Sicily in the 11th century looking for adventures and economic opportunity, but once they arrived, they found the chance for fame and fortune. Although the first Norman effort to conquer Sicily was not successful, the Norman knights quickly earned a reputation for being daring, ambitious, and resilient, bringing with them an energy that would be put to good use when they took over from the Muslims.

As the Normans gained small, informal footholds in Sicily, they likely had no idea that they were actually gathering up power for a much greater accomplishment. In 1046, the great ruler Robert Guiscard led his forces against the Muslims, and a contemporary writer provided a vivid depiction of the Norman conqueror: "This Robert was Norman by birth, of obscure origins, with an overbearing character and a thoroughly villainous mind; he was a brave fighter, very cunning in his assaults on the wealth and power of great men; in achieving his aims absolutely inexorable, diverting criticism by incontrovertible argument. He was a man of immense stature, surpassing even the biggest men; he had a ruddy complexion, fair hair, broad shoulders, eyes that all but shot out sparks of fire. In a well-built man one looks for breadth here and slimness there; in him all was admirably well-proportioned and elegant... Homer remarked of Achilles that when he shouted his hearers had the impression of a multitude in uproar, but Robert's bellow, so they say, put tens of thousands to flight."

Merry-Joseph Blondel's painting depicting Robert Guiscard

A 14th century depiction of Robert Guiscard

In 1060, he was joined by his brother Roger, and together, the two were able to take Palermo. As a reward for his valor, Roger was made the Count of Sicily, and he took advantage of the considerable wealth there by working with the indigenous people rather than obliterating their culture.[14] This, of course, was in his best interest, insofar as he needed to consolidate his power. Since he had only a few hundred knights under his command, support from the Muslims was crucial, and he chose to treat them with respect, keeping open their mosques and naming Arabic an official language on the same footing as Latin, Greek, Norman, and French.[15] Roger Guiscard started a trend of cultural hybridism that

---

[14] Mallette, 5.
[15] Norwich, Crossroads, 67.

would characterize Sicily's early development and leave an indelible mark on society.

A medieval depiction of Roger I of Sicily

A coin minted during Roger's reign that depicted him

Roger ruled Sicily until his death in 1101, and his son Roger II assumed the title in 1105 when he was only nine years old. When Roger II was crowned king on Christmas Day in 1130, the "Regno" ("kingdom") of Sicily was born.[16]

Roger II's son, William I (r. 1154-1166), posthumously earned the title "William the Bad."[17] William II had an altogether different personality from his own father. He ruled the island from 1166-1189 and earned the title "William the Good."[18]

The Normans conquered Sicily around the same time that Christians were first seizing Muslim-occupied lands in Spain and Portugal on the Iberian Peninsula. In 1070, Palermo was conquered by the Normans, and in 1072, the Christians captured Toledo. This was a major blow to the Muslims, who struggled to survive both economically and culturally under Norman rule.[19] In fact, when the Normans conquered Sicily, they not only took possession of the abundant natural resources of the island, but they also

---

[16] Jean Dunbabin, *The French in the Kingdom of Sicily, 1266–1305* (Cambridge, UK: Cambridge University Press, 2011), 19.

[17] According to Norwich, he was given this nickname two hundred years after his death, somewhat undeservedly: first, because he never managed to live up to his beloved father and second, the principle historian of his reign, Falcandus, passionately hated him. Furthermore, Norwich claims that he was apparently quite ugly, large and with a savage looking beard although no portraits of him survive. Norwich, *Crossroads,* 80.

[18] Mallette, 5.

[19] Mallette, 3.

came to control its vast cultural production and its advanced bureaucratic and cultural institutions.[20] As a result, the Normans inadvertently ended up merging Islamic art, literature and architecture in the service of a Christian king.[21] They also brought together Arabic, Greek and Latin, to develop a language of bureaucracy and of culture.[22] During the Norman rule, court poets in Sicily actually composed their poetic verses in Arabic.

12th century Sicily was a time of intense cultural exchange. The island was now inhabited by Normans, Byzantine Greeks, Arabs, Germans, and Jews, making it a paragon of cultural diversity. At the intersection of Europe, Africa, and Asia, this culture flourished and proved to be greater than the sum of its parts. In addition to the commonplace occurrence of bilingualism, it was a time when the rights of women were honored, and there were signs of respect for the environment that predated contemporary environmentalist movements by nearly 1,000 years. Sicilians during this time were uncommonly literate, so much so that 700 years later, the island's literacy rates would be markedly lower than they were during this remarkable golden age.[23]

Unfortunately, this period was relatively short lived.

---

[20] Mallette, 3-4.
[21] Mallette, 4.
[22] Mallette, 5.
[23] Louis Mendola and Jacqueline Alio, *The Peoples of Sicily: A Multicultural Legacy* (Palermo, It: Trinacria Editions, 2014).

When William II "The Good" died in 1189, he became "William the Lamented."[24] His death caused Sicily to fall into a period of confusion and discord that ultimately brought the Norman-Sicilian experimentation to an abrupt end.[25] This was due to the rise of Frederick II, who, despite being a great ruler and considered no less tolerant than his father, was much more interested in establishing strong ties between Sicily and Europe rather than the Muslim world, particularly in terms of cultural production.[26] As a result, in the late 12th century, the poets of Sicily began to write in a vernacular that was much closer to that which was being used in the Italian mainland. This ultimately produced the dialect that would come to be known as Sicilian.[27]

---

[24] Mallette, 47.
[25] Mallette, 5.
[26] Mallette, 6.
[27] Mallette, 4.

A contemporary bust of Frederick II

Italy in the 13th Century

In the 13th century, the Italian peninsula was not a unified state and in fact had not been one since the conquest of the Kingdom of the Goths by the Byzantine Empire in the middle of the 6th century. A Kingdom of Italy still existed, though it was it was confined to the north and corresponded to the territory of the Lombard kingdom conquered by Charlemagne in the 8th century. From that time, it formed a part of the Holy Roman

Empire, though from the 10th century the towns of
Lombardy began to assume prominence and autonomy
through commerce. These communes chose their own
magistrates, saw to their own defences and raised urban
militias which could even challenge the authority of the
emperor. In 1167 the Lombard League comprised most of
the cities of northern Italy including Milan, Venice,
Genoa Padua, Cremona, Bologna, Mantua and Modena
and successfully asserted their independence without
formally seceding from the Empire.

   The Lombard cities were supported by the papacy, which
ruled the city of Rome and much of central Italy. The
Pope's own dominion was a remnant of the Byzantine
conquest of Rome and gave him political and spiritual
independence. This independence was challenged by the
German emperors, who as heirs of Charlemagne claimed
the right to invest bishops and even to nominate the Pope.
But from the 11th century – about the time the Lombard
League was formed – the papacy began to reassert its
independence from the secular powers. Indeed it asserted
not only its independence, but its superiority when Pope
Gregory VII famously asserted in 1090 that the Pope was
subject to God alone and "of the Pope alone princes shall
kiss the feet."[28] He further declared that he could depose
emperors and release his subjects from their oaths of

---

[28] Proposition 9, *Dictatus Papae* https://sourcebooks.fordham.edu/source/g7-dictpap.asp.

fealty to him. The princes of the Earth had no authority to appoint bishops or regulate ecclesiastical affairs. A great power – that of the Pope, Bishop of Rome and Vicar of Christ on Earth – entered European politics.

The papal claims were not merely empty gestures: Gregory VII succeeded in deposing his enemy Emperor Henry IV and forcing him to wait three days in the freezing snow of Canossa before granting him absolution. In excommunicating the emperor, Gregory appealed to the apostle Peter, traditionally believed to be the first Bishop of Rome and hence the first Pope: "I withdraw, through thy power and authority, from Henry the king, son of Henry the emperor, who has risen against thy church with unheard of insolence, the rule over the whole kingdom of the Germans and over Italy. And I absolve all Christians from the bonds of the oath which they have made or shall make to him; and I forbid any one to serve him as king. For it is fitting that he who strives to lessen the honor of thy church should himself lose the honor which belongs to him. And since he has scorned to obey as a Christian, and has not returned to God whom he had deserted—holding intercourse with the excommunicated; practicing manifold iniquities; spurning my commands which, as thou dost bear witness, I issued to him for his own salvation; separating himself from thy church and striving to rend it—I bind him in thy stead with the chain of the anathema.

And, leaning on thee, I so bind him that the people may know and have proof that thou art Peter, and above thy rock the Son of the living God hath built His church, and the gates of Hell shall not prevail against it."[29]

Perhaps not surprisingly, the imperial power fought back, claiming that it received its power not from Saint Peter or the Pope, but from God himself, and was therefore inviolable. The clash of claims between Pope and emperor, both claiming supreme power from Christ himself, shaped the course of European politics until 1122, when the Vatican and emperor came to a forced and uncomfortable agreement. The Concordat of Worms accorded a role to the emperor in the nomination of bishops and abbots while the absolute right of appointment was left to the Pope. The right to crown the emperor remained solely with the Pope, though he was elected by a college of German princes. The chief question however as to who was the supreme prince in Christendom – Pope or emperor – remained in dispute. Pope and emperor continued to exchange blows, in particular concerning Italian affairs. From the 12th century the conflict split the northern communes into two camps: the Ghibellines (named after an imperial city in Germany) sided with the empire while the Guelfs (after the Welf

---

[29] Gregory VII, First Deposition and Banning of Henry IV
https://en.wikisource.org/wiki/Select_Historical_Documents_of_the_Middle_Ages/Book_IV/First_Deposition_and_Banning_of_Henry_IV._by_Gregory_VII.

dynasty in Bavaria) supported the Pope. Warfare ravaged Italy and divided the great families. One of the famous victims of this brutal period was Dante Alighieri, expelled from his native Florence not by the Ghibellines but by a faction of his own party, the Guelfs. Rome itself and the Papal States, which included the prosperous towns of Bologna, Ravenna, Rimini and Ancona, were not exempt from faction-driven disputes. The Pope was nominally the temporal ruler, though in reality the Papal States were in the hands of powerful Italian families. The Colonnas led the Ghobelline faction in Rome while the Orsini tended to support the Pope if he favored them.

Southern Italy – the mainland below the Papal States and the island of Sicily - was quite distinct from the rest of Italy. It was not part of the Holy Roman Empire and had been one of the last strongholds of the Byzantine Empire in Italy. The mainland, with its regional centre in Naples, was part of the Kingdom of Sicily as it had been invaded by the Normans from the island. As shall be seen the nomenclature, Sicily became somewhat complicated but suffice it to say for now that both the island and mainland made up the Kingdom of Sicily. The Lombards competed with the Byzantines in the 8th century, followed by the Muslims in Sicily and parts of the mainland in the ninth. The Normans then united Sicily and the mainland. The latest rulers were the German Hohenstaufens, the same dynasty that held the imperial crown from 1138–1254. The infant Constantine inherited the crown of Sicily in 1198 through his mother Constance, who was the descendant of Roger II, Norman king of Sicily and wife of the Hohenstaufen Emperor Henry VI. Southern Italy was then a multi-cultural society with a degree of religious toleration unknown in the north. The Hohenstaufens created a sanctuary in a part of Sicily where Muslims could continue to live and practice their religion in return for military service. Sicily was also more politically homogenous since there were fewer urban centres. The Guelf-Ghibelline divide was therefore less pronounced than in the north.

The Hohenstaufen presence in Sicily was of obvious concern to the papacy, wedged as it was with its Guelf allies between imperialists in the north and south. The Vatican was all the more outraged since the Kingdom of Naples had been a papal fief dating back to when Pope Nicholas II conferred its crown upon the head of the Norman Robert Guiscard in 1059. Rome's consternation grew when the adult king of Sicily was elected Holy Roman Emperor and took the regnal name Frederick II. He was called by his contemporaries *Stupor Mundi*, "the Astonishment of the World," not only on account of his boldness in defying the Church but for his intelligence, learning and culture, as well as for his remarkable tolerance for Jews and Muslims, whom he employed at his court and in his army.[30] Frederick declared war upon the Pope, and with the aid of men and resources from his Sicilian homeland, the emperor defeated the Guelfs in northern Italy and came close to conquering Rome.

Wolfgang Rieger's picture of a late 13th century statue of Frederick II

---

[30] Kamp, N (1995). "Federico II di Svevia, imperatore, re di Sicilia e di Gerusalemme, re dei Romani". *Dizionario Biografico degli Italiani* (in Italian). 45. Treccani.

Pope Innocent IV counterattacked by deposing Frederick II and supporting his opponents in Germany, and the once mighty ruler ended his days in 1250 clothed in the habit of a monk and pleading for the Pope's forgiveness. After his death, Germany and Italy were racked by the Great Interregnum, a civil war between Guelf and Ghibelline that lasted 67 years. A succession of rival emperors fought each other in Germany while the Papacy was left to deal with the equally chaotic situation in Italy.

After Frederick's death, the Kingdom of Sicily remained in Hohenstaufen hands, but like Germany, it was torn by the machinations of Innocent IV. The late emperor's son and regent for Sicily, Manfred, succeeded in restoring unity after defeating the papal army and suffering the excommunication of Innocent IV. He was crowned king on August 10, 1258, and in order to undermine the Pope, he assumed the leadership of the Italian Ghibellines. Florence, Spoleto, Marche, Romagna and the Lombard cities happily accepted him as their protector. As suzerain of Sicily, Pope Urban IV declared the coronation null and void and attempted to install his own nominee, Richard Earl of Cornwall, in his place. When Richard rejected the extortionate sum the Pope demanded for the favour, Urban IV instead sent envoys to Charles, youngest son of King Louis VIII of France, to negotiate his becoming king.

A 13th century illustration of Manfred

At the time, the 35-year-old prince was Count of Anjou and Provence, and his eldest brother was the reigning King Louis IX of France. France was the most powerful state in Europe and Louis one of the most prestigious and influential rulers. He had led the disastrous Eighth Crusade against Egypt, which had resulted in the defeat of his army and his own capture in 1250. But he lost no respect from the ignominy – quite the contrary. He was known to be a staunch supporter of the Pope and the Catholic Church and had supported its efforts to extirpate the Cathar[31] "heretics" in Southern France. Charles had no

claim by blood to the throne of Sicily, but his brother's
patronage and support for the papacy would ensure the
troops and money required to defeat Manfred and the
Ghibellines.

A statue of Charles of Anjou

---

[31] The Cathars held that there were two divine principles: good(spiritual) and evil (material). All matter
was therefore evil and this included the Catholic Church and civil society.

A contemporary illustration of Louis IX of France

Nevertheless, Louis forbade his brother to accept the crown of Sicily on the grounds that the second son of Frederick II, Conrad, had first claims on the throne. In doing this, Louis was uncharacteristically rebuking the Pope, and when Conrad claimed the imperial throne in opposition to Urban's candidate, William of Holland, Conrad was excommunicated. The Pope then offered the crown to another English prince, Edmund Earl of

Lancaster, the youngest son of King Henry III of England. Edmund accepted reign over Sicily on the understanding that his father would pay the enormous cost of the campaign to remove Manfred, but the English barons refused to finance an undertaking in a distant land that would not directly benefit the kingdom.

Pope Urban IV sent another delegation to Louis IX in 1263 and this time found the monarch more amenable. The Pope framed the scenario in terms of a crusade against the enemies of the Church, and the crusader-king with a reputation for piety and honour could hardly refuse such a sacred mission from the Pope. The power to declare a crusade was the most potent weapon at the Pope's disposal, and the papacy had used it frequently, notably in recent decades against the Cathars in Southern France and the pagan tribes that inhabited the southeast Baltic regions. Crusades had even been declared against Catholic Christians who fought with their bishops.[32] A crusade against Emperor Conrad IV had already been preached in England and Italy in 1255 when Edmund of Lancaster had taken up the Guelf cause, but Charles wanted the call extended to the whole of Western Christendom and specifically targeted against Manfred. The Pope agreed but insisted that Charles not assume dominion over northern Italy, nor interfere in the

---

[32] For example the peasants of Stedingen in Germany, who fought with their lord the Archbishop of Bremen over taxes and property rights in 1233.

government of the Papal States. After reaching those understandings, a preliminary treaty was agreed on June 17, 1263. Urban sent Cardinal Simon de Brion as legate to France to raise money and men for the venture while Charles took measures to secure his passage into Italy by quelling revolts in Provence and making agreements with Lombard towns.

In the meantime, Manfred had been active. After a suspicious offer to give homage for Sicily was rejected, he attacked Rome and forced Pope Urban IV to flee to nearby Orvieto. The elite citizens of Rome desired a free commune like those in Northern Italy and sought to avert the wrath of Charles of Anjou by offering him the senatorship of Rome. The Senator of Rome was that city's highest civil governor and was a medieval creation rather than a holdover from imperial Rome. The offer was indeed tempting, but rather than join the Ghibellines, Charles of Anjou pressured Urban IV to modify their agreement to allow him to accept. The beleaguered Pope could do nothing but accept, and so Rome was in effect placed in the count's hands even before he had set foot on that land.

In September 1264, Manfred's allies neared Orvieto and forced Urban to retreat again, this time to Perugia, about 50 miles to the northeast. He died either there or during the flight, and the cardinals who assembled at Perugia, divided as much by their attitude toward Charles of Anjou as by personal rivalries, took four months to elect a replacement. The supporters of the count prevailed and elected Guy de Foulques, the Cardinal of Sabina, an advisor to King Louis IX, and an inquisitor. He took the name Clement IV but was in France at the time of his election and was compelled to disguise himself as a monk in order to safely reach Perugia. He immediately confirmed the alliance with Charles of Anjou and the crusade against Manfred. The Pope again agreed to make Charles senator, and Charles agreed not to seize the imperial crown for himself, indicating he was content with Sicily.

A medieval illustration of Pope Clement IV

On May 10, 1265, Charles embarked from Marseilles ahead of the crusader army and entered Rome 10 days later. Clement IV dared not go to Rome himself since it was still firmly in Ghibelline control and he possibly suspected Charles might ally with them to make him a political hostage. Instead, he authorized a group of cardinals to confer the senatorship upon Charles on June 21, and a week later they formally invested the count with the government of Sicily. Charles spent the next six months in Rome raising money for the campaign to conquer Sicily, using church properties as surety with the consent of Clement, who had now moved his court to Viterbo. On January 5, 1266, he delegated five cardinals to formally crown Charles as King of Sicily.

Thus armed with the papal consecration, Charles of Anjou set out with his army of crusaders from France, numbering about 27,000 men.[33]

The Sicilian Vespers

Charles was anxious to crush Manfred quickly, for even with the money raised by the crusade tax and ecclesiastical properties, he could not afford a lengthy campaign. He therefore headed straight toward Naples, only to be deterred by news of Manfred mustering forces near the city at Capua. He then crossed the Apennines and headed toward Benevento, some sixty-three kilometres east of Capua and hoped to attack Naples from the east circumventing Manfred's troops. The latter rushed to Benevento and risked engaging Charles before his army was fully organized. He therefore arrived vastly outnumbered. The Battle of Benevento occurred on February 26 1266 and was a disaster for the Hohenstaufen army. As it began to fragment, Manfred refused to flee,

[33] Housley, Norman (1982). *The Italian Crusades: The Papal-Angevin Alliance and the Crusades against Christian Lay Powers, 1254-1343*. Clarendon Press, p.19.

fighting until he was killed. As an excommunicate his body could not be buried in consecrated ground and so it was left on the battlefield. However his enemies chivalrously filed past it each placing a stone upon the corpse. Clement IV, ill-disposed to forgive his enemy, had the body of the "heretic" and "Saracen "removed from Sicilian soil and cast into a river. Contemporaries described Manfred as a noble and magnanimous ruler and, like his imperial father, a patron of learning and the arts. Writing more than forty years later, Dante paid homage to him in the *Divine Comedy*, in which he is placed not in hell with his father but in purgatory.

  After Benevento support for the Hohenstaufens totally collapsed, Manfred, having no surviving son to continue the resistance, the Sicilian towns surrendered without even the threat of siege. For the time being, Charles needed to be magnanimous toward the Sicilian nobility only because he knew he would be obliged to soon antagonize them – he had promised to restore the lands of Guelph nobility who had sided with him. Furthermore, Charles had greater ambitions beyond the Kingdom of Sicily. In 1204 an army of crusaders had diverted the Fourth Crusade (against the wishes of the Pope) to Constantinople, which they conquered and made the centre of a Western, Latin Empire. But the Byzantine emperors, based in Asia Minor, counter-attacked and by

1261, Byzantine Emperor Michael VIII had reconquered Constantinople. Charles wished to raise money and an army for an invasion which would restore the Latin Empire with himself as emperor, and Sicily was merely a stepping stone. He treated his new conquest as a means to finance the venture, bringing in his own men from France and Provencal to administer the land and raise heavy taxes. The Kingdom of Sicily became a French colony, with the native population excluded from government.

Byzantine Emperor Michael VIII

Pope Clement vainly remonstrated with Charles for his

cruelties and excesses, warning him that his subjects would rebel. He had reason to be alarmed, for the Ghibellines might appeal to the last remaining Hohenstaufen, the 14-year-old Duke of Swabia, Conrad IV, known as Conradin ("Little Conrad"). Sure enough, the Sicilian nobility joined with the North Italian cities and sent an envoy to the young duke, who was under the guardianship of his uncle, Duke Louis II of Bavaria. Conrad had been titular King of Sicily until Manfred seized the throne in the mistaken belief that Conrad was dead. One of the delegates represented the Senator of Rome, Henry of Castile. Charles had resigned the senatorship and conferred it upon his cousin and ally Henry, but Henry was not content with Rome and now appeared to be plotting with the enemies of Charles. Conrad agreed to lead the counter-crusade against the French and crossed the Alps, declaring at Verona his intention to claim his inheritance in Sicily. Almost at once, Duke Louis abandoned him and returned to Germany, but Conradin remained and vowed to rid Italy of Charles of Anjou, to the great delight of the Ghibellines.

  When he heard of this, Pope Clement was furious and excommunicated the boy. Not only had the Ghibelline cause been given new impetus, but he was now obliged to again call upon Charles of Anjou, whose influence he had striven to limit. Charles and Henry of Castile had not expelled the Ghibellines from Rome, and it was for this reason Pope Clement remained at Viterbo. The papacy could not risk becoming a puppet of Charles of Anjou.

Meanwhile, Conrad was received with enthusiasm throughout Italy. Pavia, Siena, and Pisa feted him, and Henry of Castile brought Rome to his standard. His brother Frederick, who had fought with Manfred at the Battle of Benevento, landed in Sicily with a number of knights, and the island, with the exception of Palermo and Messina, rose against the French. In November 1267, Clement excommunicated Frederick, but by then most of Italy was controlled by the Ghibellines. The Pope's calls to crusade rang particularly hollow since he appeared to be the servant of Charles of Anjou, no matter how much the Vatican was striving to avoid the perception. In July 1268, Conrad, hailed as a liberator and heir to Frederick II and Manfred, entered Rome in triumph. There had been little Guelf resistance.

Confident in the belief that he was already victorious (and to be fair, there was nothing to suggest otherwise), Conrad marched south toward Naples, only to be unexpectedly met by Charles at Tagliacozzo in the province of Aquila, about 75 miles east of Rome. There, Conrad's German, Italian and Spanish knights almost defeated the Guelf army, but after initial success it split

after a man mistaken for Charles of Anjou was slain.
Charles then counterattacked, decimating the enemy and
forcing Conrad to flee to Rome.

**A medieval miniature depicting the Battle of
Tagliacozzo**

Clement IV was anxious for Charles to return south, but
he insisted on pursuing the rich and powerful Ghibellines
in Florence. He then marched to Rome, had himself
elected Senator again – which Clement confirmed - and
appointed vicars to rule in his name. He struck coins
bearing his own image rather than the Pope's, and he
began raising revenue from the Pope's lands for his
planned eastern campaign. Conrad sought refuge at the
coastal fort of Torre Astura near Romebut but was
betrayed by its owners, the Guelf Frangipani family. Most
of his retinue was massacred on the spot and he was taken
to Naples, tried for treason (a strange charge since Conrad

had never been Charles's subject), and beheaded on October 29, 1268 while his supporters of every rank and station were massacred ruthlessly.

The slaughter of a 16-year-old boy, especially one who had acted gallantly and probably genuinely in the belief he was leading a just cause, was universally condemned, and Pope Clement IV led the critics. Though he was a bitter enemy of the Ghibellines, he recognised the injustice in the death of a guileless youth and even more the dangers of a man ruthless enough to execute him. The Pope dared not move his court to Rome, and on November 23 he died at Viterbo, having never once set foot in the city of which he was technically bishop.

Clement's death was followed by a papal interregnum of almost three years, the longest period during which Rome had no bishop. There was a deep division amongst the cardinals assembled at Viterbo, many of whom were Frenchmen appointed by Urban IV and who supported Charles of Anjou. The latter naturally took advantage of the vacancy to consolidate his position in Italy, crushing the last resistance in Tuscany and the island of Sicily. At Cremona, the cities of Lombardy accepted his protection in October 1269, and with that Charles of Anjou secured his hegemony over Italy. However, the lack of a Pope hampered his ambitions for Constantinople because he needed a Pope to bless an invasion of the Byzantine

Empire.

By the summer of the following year, he felt sufficiently secure to join his brother Louis IX in a crusade against Tunisia, though it was unofficial since there was no Pope to proclaim one. The pious Louis seems to have believed that Tunisia was ripe for conversion, but Charles wanted the tribute that the possession of the caliphate would bring.

As it turned out, the venture was a military disaster. The French army was decimated by dysentery and typhoid fever, and Louis died shortly after landing. Nevertheless, the French presence was sufficiently strong for the Tunisians to sue for peace and subsequently pay Charles a yearly gold tribute.

Charles next turned his attention to the cardinals at Viterbo. In the company of his nephew King Phillip III of France, he pressured them to elect a Pope, reportedly removing the roof of the papal palace and restricting the cardinals' diets to bread and water[34]. In a token show of independence, the prelates delegated their responsibilities to a committee of six cardinals which included no pro-French members, and this group decided to elect an outsider, Theobald Visconti, a deacon who was at Acre in Palestine at the time. The election had the appearance of

---

[34] Sladen, Douglas Brooke Wheelton, and Bourne, Francis. 1907. *The Secrets of the Vatican*. Hurst and Blackett Limited. p. 48-50.

impartiality, but Theobald was a choice acceptable to the French since he had served as Archdeacon of Liege, had studied theology in Paris, and had participated in the recent French crusade. Charles met him when he arrived in Viterbo and escorted him to Rome, where he was ordained a priest, consecrated a bishop, and crowned Pope Gregory X.

The new Pope had three goals: a crusade in the east (in which he hoped the Mongols would participate[35]), peace in Europe, and the union of the Roman and Greek Churches. Charles was indifferent to the first, and Gregory's desire for peace confirmed the French hegemony, but the repair of the nearly 200-year-old religious schism between West and East was not in his interests. He made himself King of Albania in preparation for an invasion of the Byzantine Empire, but Gregory ordered him to desist because the Vatican was preparing a council at Lyons with Byzantine bishops. Byzantine Emperor Michael VIII gained a diplomatic victory over Charles by allying himself with Gregory and supporting a union, and Gregory began undermining Charles in Italy as well, recognizing Rudolf, Count of Habsburg, as King of Germany and seeking a compromise peace between the Ghibellines and Guelfs.

In 1276, Gregory X died, and during a series of four

---

[35] Gregory seems to have believed that the Mongol Khan was friendly to Christianity.

short pontificates Charles endeavoured to secure a Pope friendly to his designs. His efforts met with varying success until February 2, 1281, when the French Cardinal Simon de Brie was elected Pope Martin IV. This was the same man who was sent to France to preach the crusade against Manfred. Martin obliged the king in almost every way, primarily by excommunicating Byzantine Emperor Michael VIII, which ended any hope for a religious reunion and paved the way for an invasion in the east.

Charles now seemed unassailable, and he began to make preparations for a crusade against Michael and the schismatic Greeks. He must have believed that absolutely nothing stood in his way, and that was understandable since he was essentially the master of Italy. The Ghibellines still had their strongholds, particularly in northern Italy (Martin IV lived in Orvieto for fear of anti-French sentiment in Rome), but they certainly did not have the strength to challenge Charles. Germany at last had one universally recognized king, but he could not become emperor without coronation and could not safely enter Italy. The French continued to treat the Kingdom of Sicily as a French colony, ruthlessly raising funds for Charles's invasion of the Byzantine Empire, and by the spring of 1282 Charles's fleet was poised off the coast of Sicily, ready to attack Constantinople with the Pope's blessing.

    Seemingly out of nowhere, things began to completely unravel. Around sunset on the Monday after Easter, March 30, 1282, a large crowd of French and Sicilians gathered at the Church of the Holy Spirit in Palermo for Vespers, the official evening prayer of the Catholic Church. The mix of native islanders and their invaders had always been volatile, but so far the French had always managed to keep control. On this occasion, however, a French sergeant named Drouet dragged a native woman out of the crowd with what appeared to be dishonourable intentions. Her husband seized Drouet and knifed him while the French rushed to their dying countryman's aid. A mob of Sicilians crying "Death to the French!" fell upon them, and the rage quickly spread throughout the city. To the sound of the bells for Vespers, every Frenchman was slaughtered, including monks and clerics, the Sicilian wives of Frenchmen, and their children. It was said that if the rioters were unsure of the nationality of their prospective victims, they made them say *ciciri*, meaning chickpeas, a word the French could not perfectly pronounce. The blood frenzy spread across the entire island, and within six weeks all of Sicily was under rebel control. An estimated 4,000 French and their supporters were dead.

The Church of the Holy Spirit in Palermo

The swiftness with which the island was overwhelmed suggests that the rebellion was not entirely spontaneous and that there had been a degree of forethought and planning. Charles of Anjou naturally suspected Emperor Michael VIII as the instigator of the revolt, and certainly the Byzantine monarch immediately benefited. Charles's forces were about to invade Greece, but his plans had to be aborted to deal with the rebels.

King Peter III of Aragon, still an independent kingdom in Spain, was another suspect. His wife was Constance, daughter of Manfred, whom he regarded as the legitimate heir to the Sicilian throne, and he had welcomed Sicilian refugees into his court.

Peter III of Aragon

Regardless of who was responsible, Charles now had to use his crusader army to lay siege to Messina, while the newly liberated towns proposed to Pope Martin that Sicily become a federation of communes under the leadership of the Vatican. However, Martin VI remained beholden to Charles and refused their overtures. He also understood that abandoning Charles would potentially empower the Ghibellines and throw all of Italy into chaos.

The Sicilians then asked the help of Peter III, who was more than ready to answer their call. The Ghibellines rallied, and Italy was about to enter another phase in the bloody conflict that began with the reign of Manfred.

The War of the Sicilian Vespers

Peter III was the eldest son of King James I of Aragon and Queen Violant (Yolanda) of Hungary. He came to the throne in September 1276 when he was in his 20s, and in 1262 he had married Constance, the only heir of Manfred. He thus considered himself co-heir by right of marriage, and as early as 1268 Peter had pressed his wife's claims when the last Hohenstaufen, Conrad of Swabia, invaded Italy. In 1277 he sent John of Procida, a Sicilian refugee, to journey to Sicily, Constantinople, and Rome in search of support for his claim. At the time, Pope Nicholas III was agreeable because he believed Charles of Anjou had grown too powerful, but the election of Martin IV had since dashed all hope of papal support. Undeterred, Peter began making preparations for an invasion, and when the invitation from the Sicilian towns came, he was ready. He accepted the throne of Sicily and was promptly excommunicated by Pope Martin, but recent Popes had been using the power of excommunication so often and for such blatantly political purposes that it had lost the calamitous impact it once had.

On August 30, 1282, Peter landed with his troops at Trapani, a city on the western corner of Sicily about 250 miles from Messina, where Charles was commanding the siege. The latter did not break off to engage Peter, for he would have been trapped by the Aragonese and the rebel forces. Peter therefore captured Palermo and marched toward Messina unmolested. Charles realized he would have to fight Peter with no prospect of retreat – he was between the Straits of Messina and the city –so he crossed over to the mainland. Peter pursued him, taking most of the towns and villages of Calabria by February the following year. All the while, Admiral Roger of Lauria harried Charles's coastal defences.

Thom Quine's picture of a statue of Roger of Lauria in Barcelona

Charles was desperate and proposed a chivalric but clearly preposterous notion. He challenged Peter to single combat to decide the kingdom. Peter agreed and the date was set for June 1, 1283, but neither party had any intention of honoring the duel. That said, it bought Charles time and gave Peter an opportunity to showcase his enemy's weakness. Bordeaux was chosen as the scene of the contest, with King Edward I of England as adjudicator, but Martin IV wisely counselled Edward not to attend, so the whole arrangement collapsed.

Charles did not let his sojourn in France go idly by. He called upon a Provencal mercenary, Guillaume Cornut, to raise a force to man a fleet of 25 galleys in order to relieve the French garrison in Malta, which had been under siege from Aragonese and rebel troops since October 1282. On July 8, 1283 a fleet of about 20 Aragonese ships under Roger of Lauria sailed into the Grand Harbor of Malta at sunrise and surprised the fleet under Cornut's command. The Provencals exhausted their firepower in a frantic attack that the Aragonese weathered in their forecastles. Then they were subjected to a savage volley of arrows, after which the Aragonese galleys struck in ship-to-ship combat. By evening, Cornu had lost over 4,000 men and all but one scouting ship, which escaped to relate news of the defeat. Cornut and all his officers perished; the fortress of Castello del Mare[36] surrendered, and the Maltese swore allegiance to Peter III. The victorious fleet then sailed to the harbor of Syracuse after being celebrated by every Sicilian harbor it passed.

For almost a year there was no significant battle between the two sides, and the Aragonese and Sicilians continued to hold their fortresses in Calabria. Peter was not in Sicily himself, for King Phillip III was preparing an invasion of Aragon in support of his uncle. Moreover, he was dealing with a rebellion at home, and his brother King James II of Majorca had joined the French. In 1283, he gave his blessing to Peter's enemies by declaring a crusade against him, an act so crassly political that it excited little if any religious fervour. The Pope declared Peter deposed and gave his crown to Charles of Valois, the third son of Phillip III and Isabella of Aragon, Peter's sister.

---

[36] The same fortress overlooking the Grand Harbor that is now known as Fort Saint Angelo. It was famously defending by the Knights of John of Malta against the Ottomans in 1565.

An effigy of Charles of Valois

In the wake of that, the French army that invaded Aragon in 1284 was terrifyingly large, especially at a time when 10,000 was considered a large army. Phillip led over 100,000 troops and 100 ships from southern French ports, but the local populace resisted the invasion and the border town of Elne (now in France) valiantly held out until all its inhabitants were slaughtered and its cathedral destroyed. Phillip crossed the Pyrenees in 1285 and took Girona in April. There, Charles of Valois expected to be crowned, but since no crown could be found, the cardinal legate crowned him with his own broad-rimmed red hat. Thereafter he became known derisively as *Roi du chapeau* ("King of the hat").

   In Italy however, the French continued to suffer reversals. On June 5, 1284, Roger of Lauria had drawn out the French fleet in the Bay of Naples and destroyed it. The French were commanded by another Charles, the son of King Charles of Anjou, who had received strict orders from his father not to engage, but his impetuousness overcame him. He was taken prisoner and transported to Messina, where only imprisonment in a strong castle prevented his being lynched by the populace. Another setback occurred on January 7, 1285 when Charles of Anjou died shortly after he landed in Brindisi to make campaign preparations. His overwhelming ambition to become Emperor of Constantinople had been thwarted by the Sicilian rebellion, but he set aside whatever bitterness he may have felt to make provision for the succession, willing that his grandson, Charles Martel, would rule until his son was released. His body was buried in Naples without his heart, which was sent to Paris.

On March 28, 1285, Martin IV, staunch friend of Charles of Anjou and author of the fatuous crusade against the Aragonese, died in Perugia after a short illness. The fact that the cardinals took only four days to elect a successor is strong proof of their desire to make peace. Of the four French cardinals created by Martin, only two were present at the conclave, and even they joined in the unanimous voice for the cardinal-deacon Giacomo Savelli, who took the name Honorius IV. Honorius was about 75 and so crippled by arthritis that he had to be transported in a chair and could not celebrate Mass without assistance. He was not even a priest - he had to be ordained a priest and then a bishop before he could be crowned Pope. He was known to be more conciliatory than his predecessor and had criticized the rule of the French in Sicily, but he recognized neither the new Count of Anjou nor Peter III as King of Sicily, insisting that the crown was the gift of Rome's to bestow. In other words, the fact that Clement IV had granted it to Charles of Anjou did not mean that Charles of Anjou's heirs would inherit it. Instead, Honorius IV appointed Count Robert of Artois and Cardinal Gerald co-regents and enacted legislation to remedy the injustices inflicted on the kingdom, or at least the mainland still under French rule.

To the west in Aragon, the French army was facing disaster. The invading army was laid low by dysentery, and the people continued to resist. King Phillip himself was afflicted and a safe passage back to France was sought from Peter. Peter allowed Phillip and his entourage to cross the Pyrenees but not the bulk of his army, which was routed at the Battle of the Col de Panissars on October 1, 1285. This debacle had come on the heels of the equally disastrous Battle of Les Formigues on September 4, during which Roger of Lauria decimated the French fleet near Barcelona. The captured French were sent back to France, all with one eye gouged out. It sent the message that not even fish could freely pass through the Mediterranean without displaying the crest of Peter of Aragon.

Phillip III died of dysentery at Perpignan on October 5 1285, and about a month later, the last major player in the drama of Sicily also died when Peter III succumbed to an unknown illness after reconciling with the Church and dividing his empire between his three sons. Alfonso received Aragon, James received Sicily, and his third son Frederick served as regent for James.

With Peter dead and the French army destroyed there seemed little merit – if ever there had been – in continuing the war, so the parties agreed to a truce mediated through King Edward I of England in July 1286. Charles, the heir of Charles of Anjou, was still in captivity, and he offered to renounce the island of Sicily itself and Calabria to

James of Aragon, but Honorius objected again to being cut out of the deal. The Pope insisted he was lord of Sicily and would decide if and how it would be divided. Still, Honorius also began to negotiate with Alfonso III of Aragon before he died as the treaty was still being finalized.

Alfonso III of Aragon

With Honorius's death, the various parties' differences remained unreconciled and the war continued, with the Aragonese and Sicilians dominating the western Mediterranean by sea. Roger of Lauria was one of the finest naval commanders of his day, and the French realized that he had to be defeated if the island of Sicily were to be recovered. In the early summer of 1287, Roger sailed to the Angevin-held town of Augusta on the east Sicilian coast after receiving reports that it was to be the base for an invasion of Sicily. He recaptured the town but then realized that he had been deceived; Augusta had been a decoy, and the real invasion force was located in the Bay of Naples. There it was sheltered and protected by the artillery of the city, so Roger endeavored to entice the fleet into the open water. This would normally be a sound tactic, and Roger was an excellent admiral, but the enemy possessed about 70 galleys to Roger's 45 and had no hesitation in sailing out of the city to meet him.

To counter this, Roger withdrew out of reach, giving the appearance of retreat but remaining in formation. As the enemy fleet pursued it tended to become disorganized on account of its size. Roger then faced it, weathered the initial attack and then counter-attacked from the flanks. The battle lasted much of the day with fierce hand-to-hand fighting and the capture of 40 Angevin galleys and 5,000 soldiers. The severely mauled Neapolitan fleet returned to harbor and the invasion was thwarted. The fight was known as the Battle of the Counts because the Angevin fleet was divided into five squadrons, each commanded by a count, the chief of which was Reynaud of Avella. Also present were Jean de Joinville, the famous chronicler and biography of Louis IX, and Guy de Montfort, son of the notable Simon de Montfort (died 1265) who had ruled England and summoned the first Parliament.

The Battle of the Counts prevented an invasion, but James of Sicily could not take advantage of the crushing defeat owing to a truce arranged between the Neapolitans and Roger without the king's knowledge or consent. As a result, a kind of impasse lasted between the warring parties until the election of Pope Nicholas IV on February 22, 1288. He was chosen by only seven electors, the remainder of the cardinals having succumbed to malaria. He was a pious and peaceable man and a member of the recently founded Franciscan Order. He participated in negotiations to release Charles for 50,000 marks, the surrender of his three sons to Alfonsus III as security, and a promise to work toward a peace within three years. However, Phillip IV refused to consider peace, prompting Nicholas to absolve Charles from his oaths concerning his release. The Pope crowned him king in the spring of 1289, even though the island of Sicily still remained in Aragonese hands, after securing an oath of fealty and a promise to continue the war. The action of the allegedly peaceful Pope angered Edward I, who had brokered Charles's release, and he continued to mediate between Phillip IV and Alfonso III for a settlement.

Alfonso now invaded southern Italy, believing that Charles's Neapolitan subjects were about to overthrow him. He laid siege to Gaeta, about eighty kilometres north of Naples, but he misjudged the sentiment of the defenders. Charles Martel marched to the town's rescue and in the name of his father again attempted to negotiate peace. Peace would likely split the Sicilian realm between the island and the mainland, and as soon as Nicholas IV found out he rushed two cardinals to prevent a treaty, but no treaty was possible without the agreement of Phillip IV anyway. Nevertheless the cardinals arrived to find that Alfonso and Charles had agreed to a two year peace with the latter promising that his father would go to Phillip.

The reluctance of the papacy to join in finding a peaceful solution to the Sicilian question is hard to fathom but for Nicholas the solution was straightforward: *he* would decide who would be king, since Sicily was a papal fief. Understandably he was wary of who should rule in southern Italy. Charles II, the son of Charles of Anjou, might become the puppet of Phillip IV but better the French and their Guelf allies than the Aragonese who might well be a magnet for the Ghibellines. Forces loyal to Charles II participated in the Battle of Campaldino on June 11 1289 by which the Guelf cities of Tuscany and Romagna had vanquished the Ghibellines. Besides, a treaty between the Aragonese and French, however equitable it might be, removed the papacy from the situation as irrelevant. Nothing short of the independence of the Roman see was at stake and Nicholas needed to demonstrate that he controlled the fate of Sicily.

After lengthy negotiations, peace was finally agreed to and signed by Nicholas IV, Phillip IV, Alfonso III and Charles II of Anjou on February 19 1291. By the Treaty of Tarascon the Pope withdrew the grant of Aragon to Charles of Valois and recognized Alfonso III, who had to personally go to Rome and ask for his excommunication to be lifted. Furthermore he was required to pay a gold tribute to the Roman Church, go on crusade as penance, and withdraw material support for his brother James of Sicily. Charles II was recognized as king of a united Sicily, that is, the island itself and the mainland territory south of the Papal States. The Aragonese Crusade, which had nothing to do with religion and served only to sink the papacy's standing and embitter the powers of the western Mediterranean, was over. The Sicilian question was not however and the war for the island continued. James refused to be dispossessed, and when his brother Alfonso died not long after the Treaty of Tarascon was signed he became king of Aragon as James II, thus reuniting Sicily with that kingdom.

When Nicholas IV died in Rome in 1292, the cardinals were torn between the pro-French and pro-Aragonese factions, represented by the Colonna and Orsini families respectively. After almost two years, a well-regarded but inconsequential hermit, Peter of Morrone, wrote to the cardinals in dire tones that the wrath of God would be visited upon them if they did not elect a Pope. To the hermit's horror they returned a delegation to inform him that *he* had been unanimously elected. The cardinals evidently believed that the election of a pious octogenarian who would surely die soon would break the deadlock, but the pontificate of Peter of Morrone was a disaster. From the start, he fled and had to be dragged to his coronation. Charles II assumed the protection of the Pope, who took the name Celestine V, and persuaded him to hold court in his kingdom, at Aquila. The hermit Pope was utterly inept and allowed himself to be guided by Charles and the pro-French party, appointing Charles's men to important positions and remaining completely unaware that he was often appointing different people to the same office.

With the Aragonese party disempowered, Charles II believed he could more easily recover the island of Sicily, but Celestine V, the supposed fool whom Charles II thought he could control, dashed his hopes when, miserable and conscious of his own failings, he issued a decree proclaiming that a Pope could resign and then did so. This was Celestine's sole benign contribution to papal government in his calamitous five month.

The cardinals promptly elected Benedetto Caetani, who took the name Boniface VIII. Unlike his predecessor he was a strong if often tactless administrator who intended to reassert the primacy of the Church. Accordingly, he removed the papal court to Rome, razed the Colonna stronghold of Palestrina to the ground (killing 6,000 people), and refused to appoint any more French cardinals, thus angering Phillip IV and Charles II. The Pope further provoked the wrath of the King of France by making strong rulings concerning the extent of royal power. In particular, he forbade Phillip to tax the French clergy and its property without papal consent, to which the king responded by levying economic sanctions against the Holy See. Boniface recognized Phillip for what he was – an ambitious monarch who wanted France to dominate Europe - and believed that only a strong papacy could prevent France from effectively ruling the Church.

The problem however was that Boniface had no powerful allies. His attitude toward James II of Aragon was friendly, and when the king's brother Frederick seized the throne of Sicily the Pope enticed James into removing him by investing him with the islands of Corsica and Sardinia as well as appointing him Papal *Gonfalonier* or Standard-bearer, a mostly ceremonial office. The Pope would rather summon the Aragonese into

Italy rather than the French, and James prepared an invasion of the island of Sicily. At this point Roger of Lauria, who had left Sicily to serve for a time with Edward I of England, reappeared. But this time he fought for James II against Frederick. With his customary skill Roger defeated a fleet of Sicilian galleys at the Battle of Cape Orlando (July 4 1299) ahead of the Aragonese invasion, but the considerable advantage gained by the victory was squandered by disputes between James and his Angevin allies, and the king of Aragon returned home. Frederick then landed in Calabria, exciting unrest against the French in Naples. He made alliances with the Ghibellines in Tuscany and with the Colonna against Boniface. Boniface offered him the crown of the eastern Latin Empire if he would leave Sicily but he refused and was excommunicated.

Faced with a Ghibelline rising against him Boniface VIII reluctantly called in Charles of Valois, the same who had been crowned King of Aragon with a cardinal's hat in 1285. Like his uncle Charles of Anjou before him his ambitions lay beyond Sicily to the east. He also wished to become emperor in the east and saw Italy as a stepping-stone. Boniface VIII was prepared to give him the Byzantine Empire but not Italy. Nevertheless it became increasingly difficult for the pontiff to control events.

Charles's progress across the Alps and down the length

of Italy in 1300 harkened back to that of his uncle Charles of Anjou 35 years before, and many would have remembered the devastation that invasion had brought. The towns of Lombardy fell before him and Boniface gave him authority over Tuscany, with dubious legality, since the emperor was lord of Tuscany and there was still no crowned emperor. Florence was the chief commune of the region and was presently divided between two factions, White Guelfs and Black Guelfs. The Blacks supported Charles of Valois and Boniface while the Whites desired to keep both at a distance. Boniface would have preferred a reconciliation between the two parties that would favour his own designs, but this feat proved impossible and Charles subdued Florence with the aid of the Blacks. Though the move enhanced – temporarily – the Pope's position it embittered many of the influential families of Italy, including the Alighieri, whose most famous son, Dante, prophesized in his *Inferno* that Boniface would be tormented forever in hell. The poet also placed the unhappy Celestine in hell for resigning and allowing Boniface to be elected.

Charles of Valois departed Florence laden with honours and promises from Boniface. He was overlord of Tuscany, governor of the papal fiefs of Romagna and Ancona, as well as Papal Gonfalonier. In addition Boniface had given him his blessing for an invasion of the Byzantine Empire.

By the beginning of 1302 Charles was ready to attack the island of Sicily and laid siege to Sciacca, a port on the south-western coast. His army was formidable but took hefty losses from the plague. Also Phillip IV was no longer interested in southern Italy and needed Charles in Flanders where he was fighting the Flemish. Charles was only a pragmatic ally of the Pope and so just as pragmatically opened negotiations with Frederick of Sicily. To the fury of Boniface Phillip IV, Charles of Valois, Frederick and Charles II of Anjou agreed to a peace settlement along the lines so vehemently opposed by Nicholas IV. Sicily was to be formally separated into two kingdoms: the island and the mainland, the latter to become known as the Kingdom of Naples. By the Treaty of Caltabellotta (August 31 1302) Frederick III retained Sicily until his death, after which it would pass to Charles II of Naples or his heirs. The heirs of Frederick were to be compensated by other territories, possibly Cyprus or Sardinia. Charles paid Frederick 100,000 ounces of gold and gave him his daughter Eleanor in marriage. Frederick agreed to surrender his conquests in Calabria and Charles's son Phillip, a prisoner of the war.

  Boniface was outraged. He had been betrayed and excluded from the peace negotiations, but without allies he had no choice but to acquiesce. The seemingly interminable war over Sicily which had begun with the proclamation of a crusade against Manfred was finally over. However, the Sicilian question was still not definitively settled and the conflict between Phillip IV and Boniface VIII was coming to a dramatic head.

About two months after the Treaty of Caltabellotta Boniface VIII published the bull *Unam Sanctam*, declaring that all men of necessity had to belong to the Catholic Church in order to be saved and therefore subject to the Pope. Even the temporal powers were the servants of the Pope in all things spiritual, and when the two clashed, men were bound to obey the Pope: "Therefore, if the terrestrial power err, it will be judged by the spiritual power; but if a minor spiritual power err, it will be judged by a superior spiritual power; but if the highest power of all err, it can be judged only by God, and not by man, according to the testimony of the Apostle: '*The spiritual man judgeth of all things and he himself is judged by no man*'. This authority, however, (though it has been given to man and is exercised by man), is not human but rather divine, granted to Peter by a divine word and reaffirmed to him (Peter) and his successors by the One Whom Peter confessed, the Lord saying to Peter himself, "*Whatsoever you shall bind on earth, shall be bound also in Heaven*" etc., [Mt 16:19]. Therefore whoever resists this power thus ordained by God, resists the ordinance of God…"[37]

---

[37] Boniface VIII (1302) *Unam Sanctam*, https://www.papalencyclicals.net/bon08/b8unam.htm.

This document issued on November 18, 1302 did not contain any doctrine that was new. Pope Gregory VII had proclaimed the same thing in his conflict with Emperor Henry IV, as had his successors thereafter. Boniface was not claiming more power than the Church had previously claimed, merely reminding Europe's princes, and Phillip IV in particular, of the independence of the Church. Though it did not mention Phillip by name, he recognized in Phillip the rising power of the national monarchies and asserted the rights of the papacy. He had after all nothing left in his political armoury. The Sicilian problem had been settled, albeit incompletely, and Boniface found himself surrounded by the French.

The publication of the bull followed a tactless attempt of the Pope to browbeat Phillip and the French bishops into submission and failed spectacularly. The king ignored the bull and Boniface excommunicated him, whereupon Phillip summoned an assembly of the clergy to charge the Pope with a number of crimes, including heresy, simony, sodomy, witchcraft and the murder of Celestine V. Even as Boniface refused to acknowledge the assembly's legitimacy the king's chief councillor, Guillaume de Nogaret, invaded the Papal States on September 7 1303 and famously arrested the Pope at his palace in Anagni. The palace was plundered and the papal servants slain. Boniface himself was only saved by Nogaret's express order. This attack horrified Christendom, for the Pope was the Vicar of Christ, the representative of God on Earth, and had no worldly judge. William of Hundleby, a contemporary cleric in Lincoln, described the event:

> "[A]t dawn of the vigil of the Nativity of the Blessed Mary just past, suddenly and unexpectedly there came upon Anagni a great force of armed men of the party of the King of France and of the two deposed Colonna cardinals. Arriving at the gates of Anagni and finding them open, they entered the town and at once made an assault upon the palace of the Pope…

> "Not even the Pope was in a position to hold out longer. Sciarra and his forces broke through the doors and windows of the papal palace at a number of points, and set fire to them at others, till at last the angered soldiery forced their way to the Pope. Many of them heaped insults upon his head and threatened him violently, but to them all the Pope answered not so much as a word. And when they pressed him as to whether he would resign the Papacy, firmly did he refuse-indeed he preferred to lose his head-as he said in his vernacular: "E le col, e le cape!" which means: "Here is my neck and here my head."

"Therewith he proclaimed in the presence of them all that as long as life was in him, he would not give up the Papacy. Sciarra, indeed, was quite ready to kill him, but he was held back by the others so that no bodily injury was done the Pope. Cardinal Peter of Spain was with the Pope all through the struggle, though the rest of his retinue had slipped away. Sciarra and the captain appointed guards to keep the Pope in custody after some of the papal doormen had fled and others had been slain. Thus [were] the Pope and his nephew taken in Anagni on the said vigil of the Blessed Mary at about the hour of vespers and it is believed that the Lord Pope put in a bad night.

"The soldiers, on first breaking in, had pillaged the Pope, his chamber and his treasury of utensils and clothing, fixtures, gold and silver and everything found therein so that the Pope had been made as poor as Job upon receiving word of his misfortune. Moreover, the Pope witnessed all and saw how the wretches divided his garments and carted away his furniture, both large items and small, deciding who would take this and who that, and yet he said no more than: 'The Lord gave and the Lord taketh away, etc.'"[38]

For six days Boniface was subject to numerous indignities, including the deprivation of food and water, insults, and physical assaults. Then the people of the town repelled the invaders and rescued their Pope. He journeyed to Rome but never survived his mistreatment. He died on October 11, 1303.

The cardinals could not ignore the animosity of Phillip IV, and the new Pope Benedict XI absolved the king from his excommunication while expressing a token condemnation of Nogaret for the injuries of Anagni. Benedict XI's successor, Pope Clement V, who had been Archbishop of Bordeaux and Lyons, created nine French cardinals in 1305 and backed down from *Unam Sanctam*. He stopped short of publicly execrating his predecessor but did declare Celestine V a saint, expediting a process that normally took decades if not centuries. He collaborated with Phillip IV in the latter's desire to suppress the Knights Templar and confiscate their property and in 1309 moved the papal court to Avignon in Provence and hence within the sphere of influence of Phillip IV. Clement appointed a commission of cardinals to Rome but the city, torn by dynastic factions, was ungovernable. Thus, the fears of previous Popes of the papacy becoming a dependency of the French crown were realized, and this "Babylonian captivity of the Church"[39]

---

[38] William of Hundleby's Account of the Anagni Outrage," trans. by H. G. J. Beck, *Catholic Historical Review,* 32 (1947), pp. 200-201.

lasted 67 years. The Church had lost the independence and authority hard-won by Pope Gregory VII and his successors.

The vacuum heightened Guelf-Ghibelline tensions in northern and central Italy, and internecine strife became the norm. Clement made Robert II of Naples, the son of Charles II of Anjou, governor of Romagna and overlord of Tuscany. French influence in Italy however was challenged by Germany, which, emerging from sixty-four years of civil war when elected Henry VII of the House of Luxembourg sole king in 1308. By right of election as King of Germany Henry was also King of Italy and Emperor-elect, and he determined to restore the glory of the Holy Roman Empire. In 1311 he marched into northern Italy and was crowned king of Milan and received the submission of a number of Lombard princes and communes. Clement, under the influence of Phillip, sided with the Guelf cities in resisting him, but he could not prevent him entering Rome and receiving the imperial crown from the hands of three Ghibelline cardinals on June 29 1312. The emperor next proceeded to attack Robert of Naples, claiming sovereignty over Naples and Sicily, but died of malaria near Siena on August 24 1313. His successor Louis IV continued the war against Naples and the Papacy.

---

[39] Adrian Hastings, Alistair Mason and Hugh S. Pyper, *The Oxford Companion to Christian Thought*, (Oxford University Press, 2000), 227.

Given this state of affairs it is unsurprising that the dying Frederick III of Sicily nominated his son Peter as his successor in 1337, contrary to the terms of the Treaty of Caltabellotta. The war between Naples and Sicily reignited and continued intermittently for another 35 years. With neither side able to break the other, Queen Joanna of Naples, Frederick IV of Sicily and Pope Gregory XI came to an agreement in 1372. The Treaty of Villeneuve essentially confirmed that of Caltabellotta. It separated Sicily into two crowns, with only Joanna and her successors having the right to be called monarchs of Sicily. The island of Sicily became a sort of junior monarchy called the Kingdom of Trinacria (the ancient Greek name for Sicily) whose king was to pay tribute in the form of gold, galleys and military service. But the kingdom would not revert to Joanna and her successors after Frederick's death; the separation would be perpetual. This settlement satisfied Pope Gregory XI, for it confirmed the rights of the Holy See over both lands: Joanna was the Pope's vassal and Frederick was her vassal, and thus the unity of the kingdom was assured by a contorted fiction. Thus one hundred and six years of conflict over Sicily came to a satisfactory, if inelegant, conclusion.

In the end, the peace between Sicily and Trinacria held. In 1409, King Martin of Aragon succeeded to the crown of Trinacria by reason of his mother's claim and the two realms were united again. Alfonso V of Aragon and I of Sicily conquered Sicily (Naples) in 1442 after being named successor by Queen Joanna II. Thereafter Naples and the island of Sicily was united under the Aragonese and subsequent Spanish dynasties until it was conquered by Napoleon in 1806.

The War's Legacy

The war over Sicily was one of the pivotal conflicts of the 13th century. What began as a conflict over the sovereignty of southern Italy had, over the course of some 30 years, grown and evolved into a colossal power struggle involving the Papacy, Sicily, and all of Italy, France, Aragon, Germany and the Byzantine Empire. In the end, the only clear winner was France.

The Peace of Caltabellottga also had unforeseen consequences for the Byzantine Empire in the east. Frederick III of Sicily had employed an Italian pirate named Roger de Flor in his war against Naples and the French. De Flor began his maritime career as a member of the Templars but after expulsion for theft and apostasy took up a life as a mercenary and plunderer. Frederick made him a commander of his fleet, but when peace came in 1302, he dared not keep a band of ruthless mercenaries in his dominions and dismissed Roger. Thereupon, the latter and his band of mercenaries answered the call of Emperor Andronicus II for help against the Turks in Asia Minor. Roger and his Catalan Company, as they came to be called, were highly successful, and had they continued the Ottoman Empire might never have arisen, but Roger was ambitious and the native Greeks resentful of his ambition ensured he was assassinated in April 1305. The vengeful Catalans sacked the Byzantine Empire, which was further torn apart by its own dynastic intrigues, allowing the Turks to conquer Asia Minor with little resistance. Michael VIII had encouraged the Sicilian Vespers in 1282 to prevent an invasion of his empire, and as an indirect consequence, his successor Andronicus faced that threat from both the east and the west.

  Pope Clement IV had invited Charles of Anjou to enter Italy in 1266 to expel Manfred of Hohenstaufen from Sicily and thus defend the papacy against its Ghibelline enemies. The crusade initially succeeded but merely replaced one threat with another, for Charles and the French were a force the Popes could not contain. Moreover, Clement had failed to foresee the strength of the resistance and so committed his successors to supporting the French. In so doing the papacy lost much of its political strength and moral authority. The Aragonese Crusade was a patently political exercise intended to advance French interests which made it clear that the Pope was in effect a vassal of the French king and the Anjou ruler of Sicily. The attempt by Boniface VIII to take back authority was too aggressive and too late, and resulted in the outright annexation of the papacy. He has often been portrayed as an ambitious and tyrannical Pope – due in no small part to Dante's withering assessment and perhaps unjustly– but he recognized the danger posed by Phillip IV and drew a line in the sand. The attack upon his person at Anagni signalled the end of the papal monarchy; for some two hundred years the Popes had exercised authority over emperors and kings, but from then on they were dealt with as if they were princes like any other. Princes had made war upon the Pope before but none had dared to violate the sacred person or to challenge his right to rule the Church.

Boniface's attempts to maintain the temporal sovereignty of the Papacy over Christendom, expressed in *Unam Sanctam*, was not only opposed by the King of France but excited resistance throughout the Christian world, and since the papal teaching on the subject had not changed since Gregory VII, the disquiet would seem to reflect lost respect on account of the War of the Sicilian Vespers. Several years after Boniface's death, the legendary Italian author Dante expressed the thoughts of many when he wrote in *De Monarchia*, "I maintain, temporal power receives from spiritual power neither its being, nor its power or authority, nor even its functioning, strictly speaking, but what it receives is the light of grace, which God in heaven and the Pope's blessing on earth cause to shine on it in order that it may work more effectively…As to the proposition that the Church could give authority to the Roman government [by which Dante means the Holy Roman Empire], it must have held this power either from God or from itself, or from some emperor, or from the universal consent of all men or at least of the greater part of them; there is no other possible source for such a power in the Church; but the Church held this power in none of these ways; therefore it did not hold it."[40]

A revolution of thought had begun. Church and State were now both supreme within their spheres of influence, and from this it was but a short step to claim that princes had the right to deal with ecclesiastical matters within their own dominions. Marsilius of Padua expounded on this in his 1324 treatise *Defensor Pacis*, in which he claimed that the Pope is little more than an honorary president of Christendom who can be limited and even deposed by the emperor. National churches should be in the immediate care of the prince and the government of the universal Church should be exercised by the representatives of Christendom as a corporate body.

---

[40] Ibid, II,14.

Defensor Pacis was extraordinary for its time in that it advocated a sort of Christian republic in which everyone, including clerics and lay, were fundamentally equal. It laid out for the first time a model of popular sovereignty which, while not equivalent to popular democracy as people recognize it today, certainly broke the medieval mindset concerning the relationship between Church and State.

Marsilius's vision was actually put into effect at least in part in the early 15th century. The French captivity of the Church had emptied the Roman Church of its moral authority and it was in dire need of reform and revitalization. In 1376 Pope Gregory XI returned to Rome with this in mind but failed spectacularly. After his death eight years later, the Catholic Church in the West split when two rival Popes were elected: Urban VI in Rome and Clement VII, who resided at Avignon. For 39 years, Europe was torn with two lines of Popes (and for a time, three) hurling anathemas and declaring crusades against each other. Both churchmen and laity appealed to the Holy Roman Emperor, as the premier secular ruler of Christendom to solve the crisis, and the Emperor Sigismund facilitated a council of the Church at Constance in 1414. The assembly called on all rival Popes to resign and elected a new Pope, Martin V. The Council of Constance appealed to many of the principles of

Defensor Pacis in doing so. From then on future Popes were extremely wary of general councils of the Church and were extremely reluctant to call them. They prohibited appeals from the judgement of a Pope to a council and declared, like Boniface VIII, that the Roman bishop had no earthly judge. This remains the position of the Catholic Church to this day. Nevertheless, the doctrines of *De Monarchia* and *Defensor Pacis* remained influential throughout the 15th and 16th centuries and contributed philosophically to the Protestant Reformation. Thus, it might be said that the War of the Sicilian Vespers gave rise at least somewhat indirectly to the permanent split in the Church.

At the same time, the Guelph-Ghibelline divide continued to dominate Italian politics well into the 16th century, fueled by conflicts between France and the Holy Roman Empire. Italy was racked by a continuous state of strife, war, intrigue, murder and plunder. The sovereignty of Naples and Sicily was still being disputed in 1501 when Louis XII of France invaded Naples, citing his lineage from Charles of Anjou. As in the 13th century, the Pope, in this case Alexander VI, claimed the right of investiture and was hemmed in between French and Spanish claims. The Holy Roman Emperor and King of Germany and Spain, Charles V, finally pushed the French out of Italy in the 16th century, but the Holy Roman

Empire's imperial hegemony still did not bring unity to the peninsula. The divisions created by the Guelf-Ghibelline conflict ran deep, engendering animosities that persist in Italy to this day, and the division between north and south, the latter historically influenced by Greek, French, and Aragonese culture, is still strong. The joining of Naples and Sicily to Italy in 1861 was widely regarded as an invasion from the north,[41] and autonomist organizations still exist. In the more urbanized north, the political divisions between the cities are still evident and expressed by the concept of *campanilismo* or local patriotism.[42]

To be fair, the memory of the Sicilian Vespers itself has probably served to unite Italians more than divide them. In the 19th century, Italian nationalists recalled that the full resources of the French failed to conquer plucky Sicily, and Guisseppe Verdi wrote an opera celebrating the rebellion, *I Vespri Siciliani*, in 1855 at the height of the *Risorgomento* movement.

Ironically, it was first written in French but did not prove successful with French audiences, and indeed, according to one old legend, the French were apparently not too keen to remember Sicily. King Henry IV of France, who

---

[41] Nelson Moe (July 2002). "The View from Vesuvius: Italian Culture and the Southern Question". University of California.

[42] "Italian Culture", *Cultural Atlas*, Special Broadcasting Service, https://culturalatlas.sbs.com.au/italian-culture/italian-culture-core-concepts.

became king toward the end of the 16th century, boasted to the Spanish ambassador that he would invade Italy. "I will breakfast in Milan and dine in Rome," the monarch said. The ambassador allegedly replied, "Then, you will be in Sicily in time for vespers."[43]

Online Resources

<u>Other books about Italy by Charles River Editors</u>

Further Reading

Caven, M. 2005a. "Ducetius" in Hornblower, S. Spawforth, A. *The Oxford Classical Dictionary (3 rev. ed.)*. Oxford: Oxford University Press.

Caven M. 2005b. "The Punic Wars" in Hornblower, S. Spawforth, A. *The Oxford Classical Dictionary (3 rev. ed.)*. Oxford: Oxford University Press.

Freeman, E.A. 1891. *The History of Sicily from the Earliest Times*. In Four Volumes. Oxford: Clarendon Press.

Hornblower, S. 2005. "Peloponnesian War" in Hornblower, S. Spawforth, A. *The Oxford Classical Dictionary (3 rev. ed.)*. Oxford: Oxford University Press.

Kagan, D. 1981. *The Peace of Nicias and the Sicilian*

---

[43] *1282: The Sicilian Vespers*, Post-classical history
https://erenow.net/postclassical/howrenaissanceartistsandreformationpriestscreatedourworld/2.php.

Expedition. Ithaca, NY: Cornell University Press.

Kazdhan, A.P. 1991. "Sicily" in A.P. Kazdhan. *The Oxford Dictionary of Byzantium.* Oxford: Oxford University Press.

Lazenby, J.F. 2005. "Persian Wars" in Hornblower, S. Spawforth, A. *The Oxford Classical Dictionary (3 rev. ed.).* Oxford: Oxford University Press.

Murray, O. 2005. "Polis" in Hornblower, S. Spawforth, A. *The Oxford Classical Dictionary (3 rev. ed.).* Oxford: Oxford University Press.

Serrati, J. 2000 a. "Sicily from Pre-Greek Times to the Fourth Century" in Smith, C.J. Serrati, J. *Sicily from Aeneas to Augustus: New Approaches in Archaeology and History.* Edinburgh: Edinburgh University Press.

Serrati, J. 2000b. "The Coming of the Romans: Sicily from the Fourth fo the First Centuries BCE" in Smith, C.J. Serrati, J. *Sicily from Aeneas to Augustus: New Approaches in Archaeology and History.* Edinburgh: Edinburgh University Press.

Warmington, B.H; Wilson, R.J.A; W.N.W. 2005 "Carthage" in Hornblower, S. Spawforth, A. *The Oxford Classical Dictionary (3 rev. ed.).* Oxford: Oxford University Press.

Free Books by Charles River Editors

We have brand new titles available for free most days of the week. To see which of our titles are currently free, click on this link.

Discounted Books by Charles River Editors

We have titles at a discount price of just 99 cents everyday. To see which of our titles are currently 99 cents, click on this link.